Book 1

Nonfiction

Go, Bee, Go!

A bee sure is busy! Watch a bee do its many jobs.

Phonics Focus: *Long e* and *o* (open syllables)

Words to Learn
The word *cell* can have multiple meanings. In this book, it refers to the small space or section inside a beehive.

Phonics Focus Words		Decodable Words		High-Frequency Words	
bee	no	back	leg(s)	a	the
go	see	buzz	lick	has	wish
me	so	can	much		
		cap	not		
		cell(s)	pack		
		dash	red		
		dip	wax		
		fan	will		
		it(s)	wing(s)		
		job			

Before Reading

Ask your child what a bee's job is. Have them brainstorm a list of things they know about bees. Ask your child to flip through the pages and look at the photographs. Encourage them to share what they notice about the pictures. Ask your child to look at the cover of the book. Have them share what they notice. Ask them what they think they will read about in this book.

Explain the **Phonics Focus** of the book and go over any **Words to Learn**. Tell your child that in this book they will read many words that have *long e* and *long o* sounds in words with open syllables. Have your child say the sounds: /ē/, /ō/. Use the words from the title as examples. The words *go* and *bee* both have long vowel sounds.

During Reading

Have your child check their predictions as they read. Allow them to connect to the text and photographs through their own experiences. Encourage your child to ask questions while they read to learn, infer, and draw conclusions.

Ask your child to focus on the words that have the *long e* and *o* sounds. Have them point out words on the page that have this sound. Prompt them to think about other words they know that have these sounds.

After Reading

Ask your child to go back and check their predictions. *What did they get right? What was different from what they expected? What did they learn?* Have your child turn to specific pages they want to share about. Ask your child to recall details using questioning. *What is red? What does the bee do when it gets to a flower? Where does the bee fly back to?* Ask your child to share what they learned about a bee's job.

Book 2

Fiction

The Cake Case

Who ate the cake? Kate will take the case and find out where the cake crumbs lead.

Phonics Focus: *Long a*

Words to Learn

In the word *Kate's*, the *'s* ending shows that something belongs to Kate. In the word *new*, the *ew* makes a *long u* sound.

Phonics Focus Words		Decodable Words		High-Frequency Words	
Ace	chase	Dad	on	a	path
ate	face(s)	dish	will	and	the
bake	Kate('s)	not		is	what
cake	made			new	your
cape	take			now	
case	Zane				

Before Reading

Ask your child if they've had something go missing. Encourage them to share their answers. Ask your child to flip through the pages and look at the illustrations. Encourage them to share what they notice about the pictures. Ask your child to look at the cover of the book. Have them share what they notice. Ask them what they think they will read about in this book.

Explain the **Phonics Focus** of the book and go over any **Words to Learn.** Tell your child that in this book they will read many words that have the *long a* sound. Have your child say the sound: /ā/. Use the words from the title as examples. The words *cake* and *case* both have the *long a* sound.

During Reading

Have your child check their predictions as they read. Allow them to connect to the text and illustrations through their own experiences. Encourage your child to ask questions while they read to learn, infer, and draw conclusions.

Ask your child to focus on the words that have the *long a* sound. Have them point out words on the page that have this sound. Prompt them to think about other words they know that have the *long a* sound.

After Reading

Ask your child to go back and check their predictions. *What did they get right? What was different from what they expected? What did they learn?* Have your child turn to specific pages they want to share about. Ask your child to recall details using questioning. *What did Kate make? How did Kate find the cake? What was on Ace and Zane's faces?* Ask your child to draw a picture of their face covered with cake or another favorite dessert.

Book 3

Nonfiction

We Take a Hike

You can see so many things on a hike.
What will you see on this hike?

Phonics Focus: *Long i*

Words to Learn
In the words *bees* and *kids*, the *s* at the end of each word
makes the /z/ sound.

Phonics Focus Words		Decodable Words		High-Frequency Words	
bike	nice	bee(s)	make	a	that
five	pine	buzz	on	and	the
hike	ride	can	rock	of	thing(s)
hive	side	go	see	path	was
line	vine	in	sit		
mice		kid(s)	take		
		lake	up		
		lot	we		

Before Reading

Ask your child to talk about things they see outside. Allow your child time to share details about what they saw. Ask your child to flip through the pages and look at the photographs. Encourage them to share what they notice about the pictures. Ask your child to look at the cover of the book. Have them share what they notice. Ask them what they think they will read about in this book.

Explain the **Phonics Focus** of the book and go over any **Words to Learn**. Tell your child that in this book they will read many words that have the *long i* sound. Have your child say the sound: /ī/. Use the word from the title as an example. The word *hike* has the *long i* sound.

During Reading

Have your child check their predictions as they read. Allow them to connect to the text and photographs through their own experiences. Encourage your child to ask questions while they read to learn, infer, and draw conclusions.

Ask your child to focus on the words that have the *long i* sound. Have them point out words on the page that have this sound. Prompt them to think about other words they know that have the *long i* sound.

After Reading

Ask your child to go back and check their predictions. *What did they get right? What was different from what they expected? What did they learn?* Have your child turn to specific pages they want to share about. Ask your child to recall details using questioning. *Who goes on a hike? What do they see in a line? What do they see going up a rock?* Ask your child to share their favorite photograph in the book and tell why.

Book 4

Fiction

A Mole Home

Ever wonder who lives in a hole? Follow Mole to learn about hole homes.

Phonics Focus: *Long o*

Words to Learn

In the words *hangs* and *naps*, an *s* is added to the end of each word. This is because the verbs need to agree with the nouns *bat* and *cub*.

Phonics Focus Words		Decodable Words		High-Frequency Words	
hole	nose	bat	it	a	is
home	note	bug	log	do	that
joke	poke	cave	nap(s)	has	this
mole	tone	cub	not	have	what
		den	run		
		hang(s)	take		
		in			

Before Reading

Ask your child if they know of any animals that live in holes. Ask your child to share what they know about animal homes. Ask your child to flip through the pages and look at the illustrations. Encourage them to share what they notice about the pictures. Ask your child to look at the cover of the book. Have them share what they notice. Ask them what they think they will read about in this book.

Explain the **Phonics Focus** of the book and go over any **Words to Learn**. Tell your child that in this book they will read many words that have the *long o* sound. Have your child say the sound: /ō/. Use the words from the title as examples. The words *mole* and *home* both have the *long o* vowel sound.

During Reading

Have your child check their predictions as they read. Allow them to connect to the text and illustrations through their own experiences. Encourage your child to ask questions while they read to learn, infer, and draw conclusions.

Ask your child to focus on the words that have the *long o* sound. Have them point out words on the page that have this sound. Prompt them to think about other words they know that have the *long o* sound.

After Reading

Ask your child to go back and check their predictions. *What did they get right? What was different from what they expected? What did they learn?* Have your child turn to specific pages they want to share about. Ask your child to recall details using questioning. *Who lives in the hole? How do you think Mole felt when Raccoon asked if a hole home was a joke? What kind of home does Bat have?* Ask your child to share what kind of home in the book they would like to live in.

Nonfiction

The Dune

Have you been to a dune? Read about the fun you can have at a dune.

Phonics Focus: *Long u*

Words to Learn
The *long u* sound can sound like /yo͞o/ as in *huge*. It can also sound like /o͞o/ as in *dune*.

Phonics Focus Words		Decodable Words		High-Frequency Words	
Duke	June	at	much	a	is
dune	rule	can	run	for	off
huge	use	fun	see	I	the
		hike	so		
		hop	sun		
		it	up		
		kite	we		
		long	will		
		mile			

Before Reading

Engage your child in a discussion about dunes. Have them brainstorm a list of different activities you can do at a sand dune. Ask your child to flip through the pages and look at the photographs. Encourage them to share what they notice about the pictures. Ask your child to look at the cover of the book. Have them share what they notice. Ask them what they think they will read about in this book.

Explain the **Phonics Focus** of the book and go over any **Words to Learn**. Tell your child that in this book they will read many words that have the *long u* sound. Have your child say the sounds: /y$\overline{oo}$/, /$\overline{oo}$/. Use the word from the title as an example. The word *dune* has the *long u* sound.

During Reading

Have your child check their predictions as they read. Allow them to connect to the text and photographs through their own experiences. Encourage your child to ask questions while they read to learn, infer, and draw conclusions.

Ask your child to focus on the words that have the *long u* sound. Have them point out words on the page that have this sound. Prompt them to think about other words they know that have the *long u* sound.

After Reading

Ask your child to go back and check their predictions. *What did they get right? What was different from what they expected? What did they learn?* Have your child turn to specific pages they want to share about. Ask your child to recall details using questioning. *What did the family fly at the dune? What time of year is it? Are dunes big or small?* Ask your child to draw a picture of themselves at a sand dune.

Book 6

Fiction

A Stop at the Lake

A little girl skips to a nearby lake only to get stuck. Find out who helps her.

Phonics Focus: *Beginning s-blends*

Words to Learn

In the word *swan*, the letters *an* sound like the word *on*.

Phonics Focus Words		Decodable Words		High-Frequency Words	
scan(s)	spin	ack	nice	a	swan
skip(s)	spot(s)	at	on	and	thank
smell(s)	stem	can	red	for	the
snag	stop(s)	cut	rose	honk	to
snap	stuck	Eve	she	is	you
sniff	swim	home		now	
snip		lake			

Before Reading

Talk with your child about visiting a lake. Ask, *what might you see at a lake?* Brainstorm a list of things and create a chart with their answers. Ask your child to flip through the pages and look at the illustrations. Encourage them to share what they notice about the pictures. Ask your child to look at the cover of the book. Have them share what they notice. Ask them what they think they will read about in this book.

Explain the **Phonics Focus** of the book and go over any **Words to Learn**. Tell your child that in this book they will read many words that have *beginning s-blends: sc, sk, sm, sn, sp, st, sw*. Use the word from the title as an example. The word *stop* has a *beginning s-blend*.

During Reading

Have your child check their predictions as they read. Allow them to connect to the text and illustrations through their own experiences. Encourage your child to ask questions while they read to learn, infer, and draw conclusions.

Ask your child to focus on the words that have *beginning s-blends*. Have them point out words on the page that have this sound. Prompt them to think about other words they know that have *beginning s-blends*.

After Reading

Ask your child to go back and check their predictions. *What did they get right? What was different from what they expected? What did they learn?* Have your child turn to specific pages they want to share about. Ask your child to recall details using questioning. *How does Eve get to the lake? Who does Eve meet at the lake? How does her new friend help her?* Ask your child to talk about a time they helped someone, or someone helped them.

Book 7

Nonfiction

Slime Club

It is time for slime club! Find out how these kids have fun with slime.

Phonics Focus: *Beginning l-blends*

Words to Learn

In the word *glue*, the letters *ue* make the *long u* sound.

Phonics Focus Words		Decodable Words		High-Frequency Words	
bling	flop	dish	mix	a	is
blob	glam	fun	much	and	my
clock	glass	get	pal(s)	are	some
club	slime	in	see	for	the
flip		it	so	glue	to
		long	take	here	with
		make	time		
		me			

Ask your child to share if they've ever played with or made slime. Ask, *what does slime look/feel like?* Ask your child to flip through the pages and look at the photographs. Encourage them to share what they notice about the pictures. Ask your child to look at the cover of the book. Have them share what they notice. Ask them what they think they will read about in this book.

Explain the **Phonics Focus** of the book and go over any **Words to Learn**. Tell your child that in this book they will read many words that have *beginning l-blends: bl, cl, fl, gl, sl.* Use words from the title as examples. The words *slime* and *club* have *beginning l-blends*.

During Reading

Have your child check their predictions as they read. Allow them to connect to the text and photographs through their own experiences. Encourage your child to ask questions while they read to learn, infer, and draw conclusions.

Ask your child to focus on the words that have *beginning l-blends*. Have them point out words on the page that have this sound. Prompt them to think about other words they know that have *beginning l-blends*.

After Reading

Ask your child to go back and check their predictions. *What did they get right? What was different from what they expected? What did they learn?* Have your child turn to specific pages they want to share about. Ask your child to recall details using questioning. *What do the children do in their club? What is one thing you need to make slime? What is one thing you can do with slime?* Ask your child to imagine they made slime. Ask your child to draw a picture of their slime.

Book 8

Fiction

Bree's Crib

It is time for Bree's nap, but she is not sleepy. Find out what Bree does instead of taking a nap.

Phonics Focus: *Beginning r-blends*

Words to Learn

In the word *play*, the letters *ay* make the *long a* sound.

Phonics Focus Words		Decodable Words		High-Frequency Words	
Bree('s)	Fred	am	on	for	my
crab	frog	bang	set	from	to
crib	grab	in	side	I	with
drag	Gram	it	time	is	
drive	grip	me	top		
drop	truck	nap	up		
drum		no			

Before Reading

Talk with your child about when they used to take a nap. Ask your child to flip through the pages and look at the illustrations. Encourage them to share what they notice about the pictures. Ask your child to look at the cover of the book. Have them share what they notice. Ask them what they think they will read about in this book.

Explain the **Phonics Focus** of the book and go over any **Words to Learn**. Tell your child that in this book they will read many words that have *beginning r-blends: br, cr, dr, fr, gr, tr*. Use the words from the title as examples. The words *Bree* and *crib* have *beginning r-blends*.

During Reading

Have your child check their predictions as they read. Allow them to connect to the text and illustrations through their own experiences. Encourage your child to ask questions while they read to learn, infer, and draw conclusions.

Ask your child to focus on the words that have *beginning r-blends*. Have them point out words on the page that have this sound. Prompt them to think about other words they know that have *beginning r-blends*.

After Reading

Ask your child to go back and check their predictions. *What did they get right? What was different from what they expected? What did they learn?* Have your child turn to specific pages they want to share about. Ask your child to recall details using questioning. *Who put Bree down for her nap? Who is Fred? What instrument does Bree play?* Ask your child to recall the sequence of events in the story by using props to retell the story.